What we
already know

What we already know

Richard Page

Ffotogallery

Sleeping Partner

Foreword

Richard Page is not the first, and he won't be the last practitioner to use the optical properties of the large-format camera to skew depth of field and introduce a degree of subversion into the photographic picture plane. In fact, in recent years a considerable number of photographers and artists – across the globe – have harnessed this technique, or variations of it, to differing degrees of success. For the most part, this reworking of the image has tended to create a fascinating pictorial space reminiscent of a world in miniature, where real objects take on the mantle of diminutive models. People and places, buildings and spaces are literally transformed in front of our eyes into playful and arresting scenarios. Visually, this sleight of hand can produce very seductive and pleasurable mise-en-scènes, generating a vibrant aesthetic in its own right. Richard Page's rendition of this discrete 'genre' appears to take the conceit one stage further, in a way that, I would argue, places his practice at the service of a wider, more profound, agenda. The environments that he chooses to work with are largely prosaic: sites on the edges of suburban housing estates, anonymous industrial parks, shopping centres and peripheral locations that are devoid of a sense of communal ownership. This is by no means new photographic terrain as such, but the ambience of these marginal places, charged with the peculiarities of the pictorial distortion, reveals a dark psychological underpinning and inherent drama in the photographer's illuminated lightbox works. The sensibility and sense of foreboding embodied in these images of places we know, or think we know, eloquently foregrounds our increasingly voyeuristic culture of anxiety, where our understanding of the urban space around us is progressively defined, not by empirical experience, but by the furtive presence of the surveillance camera image, mobile phone grabs and the spectacle of 'reality' programming in our omnipresent and image-saturated news media. Perhaps, most alarmingly, as Mark Bolland concludes in his engaging essay which prefaces the images in this book – and as Richard Page's photography bears witness – the character of the urban landscape itself has become alien and inhospitable, as a direct result of draconian attempts by the state to control, scrutinise, police and 'make safe' public and private space.

Christopher Coppock, Director, Ffotogallery Wales

The Decoy

Mark Bolland

A little over fifty years ago Ludwig Wittgenstein famously suggested that "…we regard the photograph […] as the object itself (the man, landscape, and so on) depicted there. This need not have been so. We could easily imagine people who did not have this relation to such pictures. Who […] would be repelled by photographs."[1] Wittgenstein's suggestion still seems intriguing even if it is rather less plausible now. This is perhaps because it is so difficult to imagine someone for whom photographs are alien (although such people probably still exist). In a world structured by and consisting of photographs, other kinds of pictorial images might be regarded as strange and repelling or, perhaps, beautiful and compelling, in a way that the majority of photographs never can be. We generally accept the reduction of reality into photographs and take it for granted without experiencing the resistance that Wittgenstein describes. In fact, we are so accustomed to photographs that we pass the majority by without consideration, or even a second look. This is one of the challenges that face the contemporary photographer; how do you get people to scrutinise something they see all the time? Especially if the subject matter, as well as the medium, is 'everyday'.

The idea that a photograph might stop, shock or repel us seems almost like a contradiction in terms. Photographs are so widely used and disseminated partly because they have the appearance of the world they depict; their means of coming into being is analogous with our vision, and this convinces us in a way that overrides our scepticism about their reductive nature. As Jean Baudrillard reminds us, "to make an image of an object is to strip the object of all its dimensions one by one: weight, relief, smell, depth, time, continuity and, of course, meaning".[2] We do not normally strip the object of its legibility, though. This is what led Roland Barthes to famously describe photographs as having the appearance of being "a message without a code".[3] Photographs disappear to reveal their subject and we conventionally regard them, as Wittgenstein suggests, as transparent windows through which we view the world: they then perpetuate the myth of the picture as a window, the photograph as a 'mirror of nature'. Of course photographs have changed since Wittgenstein's time: they are now more than likely to have colour, even if it is grossly exaggerated, they might also have a similar scale to their referent. All of which makes them, increasingly, just another part of the landscape.

Installation of works, *Jerwood Photography Awards 2004*, Jerwood Space, London

It seems impossible, looking back from the image-saturated 21st century to imagine the shock, wonder and delight that the viewers of the first photographs must have felt. Such a time seems almost as far away and as inconceivable as trying to imagine what it was like to walk into a church in Rome in the early 1600s and find yourself face to face with Caravaggio's hyper-realistic figures that seem to emerge from the darkness as if they are alive. Perhaps one of the few shocks left to the photographic is that of the illegible, or nearly illegible, image, and perhaps this is one of few ways in which a photograph might compel us to look for a while. Certainly, the majority of photographic disciplines are necessarily concerned with legibility, with precision and clarity and it is the luxury of images intended for an art context to be able to stray from these descriptive duties.

The majority of photographs that we encounter might be referred to as 'déjà lu',[4] that is, they are 'already read' – we are able to read them so quickly because, the chances are, we have seen them before. Or, rather, we have seen something similar enough to make them easily legible. Photographs do not just induce a feeling of déjà vu because they re-present the world, but also induce one of 'déjà lu' because they are *generic*, in spite of the fact that each photograph represents something specific. Disturbing or disrupting a particular recognised genre of image is another strategy that is available to the critically engaged contemporary photographer.

Richard Page's photographs deliberately provoke the anxiety that is induced by the almost illegible image and the disrupted genre, potentially making us all people for whom these images are alien, even whilst retaining enough clarity and detail to show us something familiar and recognisable. What we see is the peripheral landscape of urban and suburban Britain, often in twilight or at night. Yet these are not topographical photographs; the viewpoints are often unusual and a great deal of information is withheld or excluded. We see generic suburbs of mass-produced houses and anonymous 'in-between' places through trees, along paths and around corners. Page's obfuscations imply that something is happening in the non-places he photographs, but he never quite discloses what that might be. It is the uncertainty that this provokes in us as we view his pictures that is perhaps the subject of Page's work, and it is wholly appropriate that in

The Concierge, 2006

our current 'culture of fear' we are made to feel uneasy by pictures of ordinary places, by 'what we already know'.

This disarming effect is produced by a combination of carefully chosen locations and a kind of perversion of the architectural photographer's trick of tilting the back of a plate camera to 'correct' distortions, such as those caused by looking up at a subject. Page's choice of locations defies the normal modus operandi of the landscape photographer. Even the recent vogue for 'non-places' in contemporary photography does not quite prepare us for the startling lack of obvious subject matter in these images: car parks are deserted, paths unused, buildings anonymous, and – unusually in a culture of clutter – walls are devoid of signs and adverts. This emptiness is unsettling in itself, seeming contrary to the contemporary landscapists' agenda of studying 'the process of settlement',[5] and this is emphasised by the photographer's manipulations to the film plane of his camera.

Rather than using it to 'correct' distorted space, Page uses his camera to blur *and actually distort* space and objects.[6] In this manner, he creates a field of focus which is diagonal or perpendicular to the image plane, rather than parallel to it. These appear as slices of clarity that cut through an otherwise blurry and indistinct image. Using this process, Page directs us towards a particular part of the image in the same way that a 'focus pull' directs our attention towards a particular part of the frame in a movie. This selective focus seems unusual because we have become accustomed to photographs which aim for maximum clarity, particularly landscape photographs: so valued is such precision that the large-format camera, small aperture combination that produces it, is even alluded to in the name chosen by one of the most famous assemblies in the history of landscape photography, 'Group f/64'.[7] This has not always been the case though, and lenses, cameras and film have been developed especially to achieve this lucidity. In some respects the natural mode of the camera, if there can be such a thing, is the shallow depth of field produced by a large aperture and a simple lens. In this way Page's images are closer to the magical projections thrown on to the ground glass of a camera obscura or to the overtly manipulated and retouched images of turn of the twentieth century 'Pictorialist' and 'Impressionist' photographers than they are to recent conventional landscape

The Reconstruction, 2006

photographs. Like those of the Pictorialists, Page's pictures are highly aesthetic, and this effect is heightened by his mode of presentation: they are displayed as transparencies on lightboxes and, as such, are beautiful, auratic and highly seductive. The glow of the lightbox can entrance us and suck us into the image; we study the slices of clarity in each picture, only to find that, the more we look, the more artificial what is depicted seems. Computer designed faceless offices and archetypal 'Barratt'-style houses already look simulated, resembling film sets or models, and this effect is greatly magnified in Page's pictures.

Perhaps an even more apposite parallel than that with the Pictorialists might be found, though. We should trace Page's work, as well as that of other contemporary artists who are purveyors of suburban spookiness, such as Gregory Crewdson, Peter Doig and George Shaw and others, to their origins in 'B' movies; specifically horror films and made-for-TV crime thrillers. These represent the cultural arena that most commonly utilises Freud's definition of the uncanny, as filtered through Hitchcock, wherein the most familiar sights (and sites) are rendered grotesque or disturbing by their sudden unexplainable unfamiliarity or the inanimate is suddenly rendered terrifying by becoming animate. Such films, and the artworks they influence, are not in themselves uncanny as they are obviously fictive, but these kinds of movies have made suburbia the place where the homely is rendered *unhomely*, where the everyday is infused with a sense of menace.

Currently, this notion of peril lurking in the quotidian is not the exclusive domain of the fictions and fantasies of art and the movies, but belongs also to those institutions who claim to be on the side of 'facts' and 'truth': the news media and governments are equally likely to participate in engendering suspicion where there was none, and in casting the ordinary as potentially malevolent. After all, since September 2001, this is the age of security anxiety. We, in the 'West', are both more secure than ever before and more anxious, especially in the suburbs, it seems, where burglar alarms and 'neighbourhood watch' schemes are commonplace. We live in a paranoid culture of endless signs, constant instructional announcements and ubiquitous CCTV, of razor-wire fences around school playgrounds and concrete barriers around parliament. We are constantly told to be 'on guard' and 'on the lookout' for 'suspicious' behaviour and packages, and we are

Human Resources #2, 2006

increasingly expected to police ourselves and each other whilst we have our liberties eroded by the governments which are apparently trying to protect us. In such a culture, cameras are both the key agent of 'security' and (mis)information and also one of the first things to attract suspicion: to attempt to photograph the ordinary, particularly at night, is to attract suspicion, one is immediately assumed to be 'casing' something with a view to coming back later to bomb or burgle it, or else one is cast as being out to gain some voyeuristic pleasure by observing something or someone through the mechanical eye of the camera. Unless you have been in such a situation, it is difficult to imagine oneself in the position of 'other' in this context. This is precisely the success of Richard Page's photographs; we suddenly find ourselves in this position, feeling slightly uneasy, unsure where we are but convinced we've been there before. Like the somnambulist who awakes night after night in odd places without knowledge of how they arrived there; we feel dislocated as we try to focus on our surroundings and we become aware that we are vulnerable and exposed. The world is simultaneously familiar and alien, banal and fascinating, revealed in a new light and obscured. Fantasy and reality converge in a way that suggests something that was previously repressed might be about to 'come to light', but this resolution is perpetually withheld and each image denies any specific narrative, leading us back to search for answers in 'what we already know' about these strangely familiar scenes and their mode of depiction.

Photographs and other one-point-perspective pictures predominate our image-saturated culture because they effectively place us, as viewers, in the centre of the image and, in doing so, paradoxically make us both the centre of the depicted world and exclude us from it. Richard Page's photographs serve to remind us of this phenomenon and invest it with new resonance; our exclusion from the world of the image becomes a metaphor for the ways in which we are induced to feel repelled by, or excluded from, our everyday environment as it is 'made strange' by impersonal 'redevelopment' that attempts to control and regulate our behaviour, aided and abetted by signs and surveillance technology, and is simultaneously politicised even further by being cast as the potential locus of that which we are told to fear. Presently, photographs are not generally regarded as inhuman, but the rest of the landscape is increasingly so.

Notes

1. Ludwig Wittgenstein, *Philoshophical Investigations Part II* (Basil Blackwell, 1967).
2. Jean Baudrillard, "For Illusion is Not the Opposite of Reality", *Photographies 1985–98* (Hatje Cantz, 1999).
3. Roland Barthes, "The Photographic Message," *Image / Music / Text* (Fontana, 1977).
4. The phrase is Roland Barthes'.
5. See Jeff Wall, "About Making Landscapes", T. De Duve et al. (eds), *Jeff Wall* (Phaidon, 1996).
6. It should be mentioned that Page is not the only contemporary photographer to use this and other similar techniques. Others include Olivo Barbieri, Miklos Gaál and Jean-Luc Mylayne.
7. Group f/64 was founded in 1932 by Ansel Adams, Imogen Cunningham, Edward Weston, Willard van Dyke and several others.

Mark Bolland is an artist and writer, and a Lecturer in Photography at University College for the Creative Arts in Farnham. Since graduating from the Royal College of Art in 2004 he has written regularly for *Source* and has contributed to *Portfolio*, *Photoworks* and *Afterimage*. He is currently researching the prehistory of photography and is exhibiting new photographs in *Oil & Silver: 5 Dialogues between Photography and Painting* at Hoopers Gallery, London in 2007.

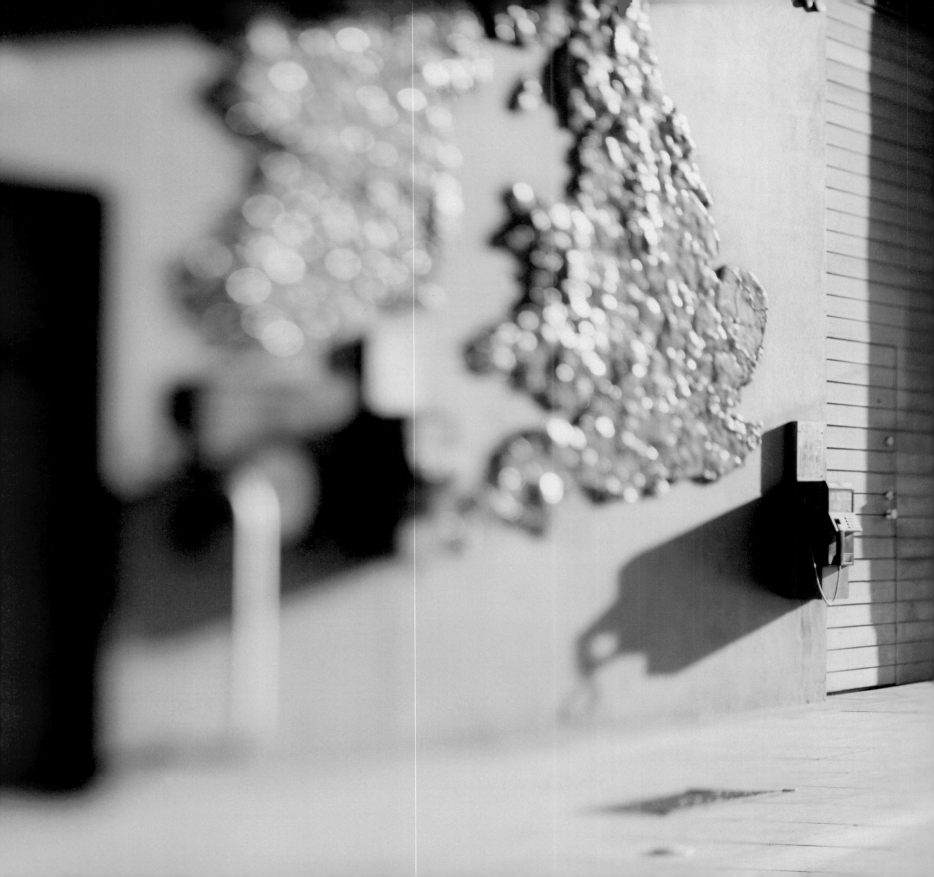

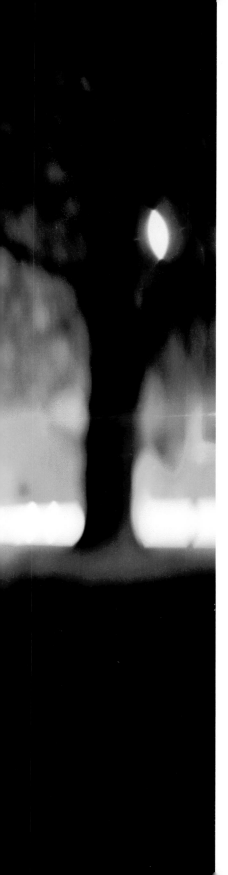

List of works

All works are presented as Fujitrans prints on perspex in lightboxes of 13 cm depth.

1. *Sleeping Partner*, 2006 [76 × 100 cm]
2. *Suburban Exposure #6*, 2004 [40 × 50 cm]
3. *A True Story*, 2006 [76 × 100 cm]
4. *Suburban Exposure #5*, 2004 [50 × 40 cm]
5. *The Wrong Location*, 2005 [76 × 125 cm]
6. *Automated Response*, 2006 [60 × 30 cm]
7. *The Decoy*, 2006 [100 × 110 cm]
8. *Suburban Exposure #1*, 2003 [50 × 60 cm]
9. *Zone #1*, 2005 [75 × 75 cm]
10. *Human Resources #3*, 2006 [25 × 28 cm]
11. *Suburban Exposure #2*, 2003 [120 × 60 cm]
12. *Suburban Exposure #4*, 2003 [75 × 75 cm]
13. *Suburban Exposure #3*, 2003 [25 × 25 cm]
14. *Zone #3*, 2006 [76 × 100 cm]
15. *Risk Assessment*, 2006 [50 × 40 cm]
16. *Stage Fright*, 2005 [125 × 100 cm]
17. *Conspiracy Theory*, 2005 [40 × 75 cm]
18. *The Blind Spot*, 2003 [diptych: 75 × 90 cm each]
19. *Human Resources #1*, 2005 [100 × 150 cm]
20. *The Glitch*, 2006 [76 × 125 cm]

1

2

3

4

5

6

7

8

9

10

11

12

13

14

15

16

17

18

19

20

Richard Page

Education

2001–2003   MA Photographic Studies – University of Westminster, London, UK
1993–1996   BA (Hons) Film & Photography – University of Wales College, Newport, Wales, UK

Solo Exhibitions

2003   *Landscapes from the Tryweryn Valley*, Maidstone Museum & Art Gallery, England, UK
2002   *Landscapes from the Tryweryn Valley*, Rhyl Museum, Wales, UK
2000   *Landscapes from the Tryweryn Valley*, Altena Museum & Art Gallery, Germany
1999   The Royal Photographic Society, Bath, UK

Group Exhibitions

2006   *Relocation*, Plymouth School of Art & Design, Plymouth, England, UK
2005   *Coagulation*, TactileBosch, Cardiff, Wales, UK
        The Jerwood Photography Awards 2004, The Jerwood Space, London, UK
2004   *Arts & Crafts Exhibition*, National Eisteddfod of Wales, Newport, Wales, UK
        Twenty Shadows, Focal Point Gallery, Southend-on-Sea, England, UK
2002   *Ha Ha: Margam Revisited*, Ffotogallery, Cardiff, Wales, UK
        Capel Celyn – The Artist's Response, Canolfan y Plase, Bala, Wales, UK
        But Still…, G39, Cardiff, Wales, UK
2001   *A470*, Oriel Mostyn Gallery, Llandudno, Wales, and Chapter Arts Centre, Cardiff, Wales, UK
        Coast, ArtSway Gallery for Contemporary Arts, Hampshire,UK
2000   *Arts & Crafts Exhibition*: National Eisteddfod of Wales, Llanelli, Wales, UK
        Afon/River, Oriel Mostyn Gallery, Llandudno, Wales, UK
1999   *Ffotoannual*, Ffotogallery, Cardiff, Wales, UK

Selected Articles / Reviews

2006 Francesca Genovese, 'Richard Page: Suburban Exposures', *Re:Imaging Wales* (November 2006)

2005 Diane Smyth, 'Jerwood Prize Rewards Rising Stars', *British Journal of Photography* (5 January 2005)

2004 Amna Malik, 'Jerwood Photography Awards 2004', *Portfolio* (No. 40 / December 2004)
Mark Bolland, 'Twenty Shadows, Andy Lock and Richard Page', *Source* (No. 39 / Summer 2004)
Sarah Browne, 'Blanchardstown', *Circa* (No. 110 / Winter 2004)

2003 Iwan Bala, 'The Trauma of Tryweryn', *Here & Now; Essays on Contemporary Art in Wales* (Seren, 2003)

2002 Heather Phillipson, 'Blinc and … But Still', *Artists' Newsletter* (March 2002)

2001 Caroline Juler, 'On the Road', *Art Review* (June 2001)

2000 Tudur Dylan Jones, 'Lluniau Tryweryn', *Taliesin* (No. 110 / Winter 2000)
Caroline Juler, 'The Green, Green Grass of Home', *The Royal Academy Magazine* (No. 68 / Autumn 2000)
Penny Fray, 'Ghosts of a Lost Landscape', *The Daily Post – Liverpool & North Wales* (23 June 2000)

1999 Jennie Savage, 'Landscapes from the Tryweryn Valley', *Skip Magazine – Contemporary Art in Wales* (August / September 1999)
Jonathan Jones, 'Landscapes from the Tryweryn Valley', *The Guardian – G2* (14 June 1999)

RICHARD PAGE: WHAT WE ALREADY KNOW
Published by Ffotogallery Wales Limited

FFOTOGALLERY
c/o Chapter Arts Centre, Market Road, Cardiff CF5 1QE, www.ffotogallery.org
Ffotogallery is supported by the Arts Council of Wales & Cardiff County Council

ISBN: 978 1 872771 68 7

Editor: Christopher Coppock
Design: Tony Waddingham/Oblique
Copy proofing: Lis Edwards

Cover printed on: 135gsm Magno Star paper
Text printed on: 150gsm Artic the Volume paper
End papers: 170gsm Popset Pistache

Printed by Antilope Printing, Industriestraat 5, I.Z. Hagenbroek, 2500 Lier, Belgium
Published in an edition of 600, January 2007

This monograph was published to coincide with an exhibition of the same name at
Ffotogallery@TurnerHouse, Plymouth Road, Penarth CF64 3DM, Wales
13 January – 4 March 2007.

Richard Page received a *Project Grant for Individuals* from the Arts Council of Wales in
2006 to develop new work and support the production of works for the exhibition.

Ffotogallery would like to thank the Faculty of Art & Design at Swansea Institute of
Higher Education for their financial contribution to the book.

Front cover: *The Decoy,* 2006

CEFNOGI CREADIGRWYDD
CYNGOR CELFYDDYDAU CYMRU
THE ARTS COUNCIL OF WALES
SUPPORTING CREATIVITY

SWANSEA INSTITUTE
ATHROFA ABERTAWE

A Member of the **University of Wales**
Aelod o **Brifysgol Cymru**

Noddir gan
Lywodraeth Cynulliad Cymru
Sponsored by
Welsh Assembly Government